Women on Success

Character Building Wisdom

*Compiled by the staff at the
American Success Institute*

THE ACTION PRINICIPLES®, THE CATHOLIC ACTION PRINCIPLES™, THE SHAOLIN ACTION PRINCIPLES™, MASTER SUCCESS™, AFRICAN-AMERICANS ON SUCCESS ™, POSITIVE MENTAL ATTITUDES™, WINNING WITH SMALL BUSINESS™, TENGA UNA ACTITUD MENTAL POSITIVA™, WOMEN ON SUCCESS™, SPORTS LEGENDS ON SUCCESS™ and ATTITUDES MENTALES POSITIVES™ are all trademarks of the American Success Institute, Inc.

Educational and motivational materials from the American Success Institute are available at special discounts for bulk purchases. For additional information, contact:

American Success Institute, 5 N. Main St. Natick, MA 01760
www.success.org
Phone: 1-800-585-1300
e-mail: info@success.org

Cover, book design, typography, and electronic pagination by Painted Turtle Productions, Newton, MA. www.paintedturtle.com

Printed in the United States of America

ISBN 1-884864-07-4
Library of Congress Catalog Card Number 2004116509

I am only one; but still I am one. I cannot do everything, but still I can do something. I will not refuse to do the something I can do.

Helen Keller, Writer

Introduction

We hope that you will enjoy and be inspired by the quotes that we have selected for this book. They are words from a broad range of perspectives. The ideas and advice can help us all to better cope with the challenges we face in pursuing careers, raising families, and finding personal peace and fulfillment.

For the most part, the quotes are from women of prominence, but the sentiments enjoy a universality that represents the practical advice that we have all already heard from our mothers, teachers, and sisters.

For when you prepare your next speech, when you simply need a boost in your day, or when you become the advice giver, you now have a ready reference.

Please continue to pass along these positive affirmations of successful living. If you have a favorite quote for our women's success archive, please join the Women's Discussion Forum on Success.org.

How To Use This Book

You can read through this book in one sitting or many sittings, or, even better, you can treat it as a "quote-a-day" inspirational guide. Its handy size allows you to keep it nearby: in a pack, purse, glove compartment or desk drawer. Each day, besides simply reading a quotation, you can think about it and live with it. Pay attention to your thoughts and actions during the day, and see how they can relate or already do relate to the quotation.

These books are priced at one dollar each to encourage distribution. Teachers, counselors, managers, group leaders, parents or anyone can use these inspiring words to initiate positive conversations. If you have a friend in need of encouragement, hand her a book. Consider donating copies of this book to women's shelters and support groups.

Use this book in an active way. Start

writing down your own thoughts. Make notes expanding on what others have said, and come up with your own original thoughts which you can write down and use to guide yourself toward your goals. Perhaps, in addition to leading a successful life yourself, someday your words might even help lead others along the road to success. This is the spirit of *The Action Principles*®. This is the spirit of *Women on Success*™.

On The Cover

QUEEN NOOR: Her Majesty Queen Noor was born Lisa Najeeb Halaby to an Arab-American family distinguished for its public service. A Princeton graduate, she became Queen of Jordan in 1978. As Queen, she has initiated, directed, and sponsored projects and activities in Jordan to address specific national development needs in the areas of education and human rights.

RUTH BADER GINSBERG: – Justice Ginsberg was appointed to the Supreme Court by President Clinton in 1993. Known for her scholarship, Justice Ginsberg was the first woman to be selected for Law Review at both Harvard and Columbia Law Schools. Justice Ginsberg has championed many women's causes from the High Court.

SANDRA DAY O'CONNOR: – Justice O'Connor is the first woman justice to sit on the Supreme Court. President Reagan appointed her to the High Court in 1981. She is a graduate of both Stanford and Stanford Law School. She is a known coalition builder, finding practical solutions to complicated problems.

BARBARA JORDAN: [1936 – 1996] – In 1972, Barbara Jordan became the first black woman to be elected to the Congress from the South. She was a graduate of Boston University Law School. Her efforts in sponsoring bills to help the disadvantaged are well documented.

DR. MARGARET MARY FITZPATRICK, S.C.: She is President and CEO of St. Thomas Aquinas College in Sparkill, New York. She is a Sister of Charity and earned her Doctorate at Columbia University. A dedicated educator and visionary, Dr. Fitzpatrick has devoted her career to improving the higher educational system in the United States.

The Women's Action Principles™

We appreciate that many of our nation's government, judicial, business, sports and religious leaders have lent their words and support to our ever-expanding international educational efforts. From Colin Powell to Queen Noor to Maya Angelou to Cardinal Egan to Reverend Schuller to General Myers to Donald Trump to Ted Koppel and to many others, we are grateful. All six American Presidents covering the last three decades have written Action Principles®. You can read their words of inspiration in the free Special Editions of *The Action Principles*® on Success.org.

- The Presidential Action Principles™
- The Washington Action Principles™
- The Shaolin Action Principles™
- The Armed Services Action Principles™
- The Catholic Action Principles™
- The Celebrity Action Principles™

The complete list of Women's Action Principles can be found on Success.org. A selection of Women's Action Principles™ follows.

★

SANDRA DAY O'CONNOR, ASSOCIATE JUSTICE OF THE U. S. SUPREME COURT

Aim High

The habit of always doing your best regardless of how unimportant the task is a habit of the successful. As Abraham Lincoln once said: "I always prepared myself for the opportunity I knew would come my way." As his career attests, devotion to excellence in all things, even when it seems that the world will little note nor long remember the small tasks in which you find yourself engaged, can have its rewards.

SANDRA DAY O'CONNOR

The individual can and does make a difference, even in this populous, complex world of ours. The individual can make things happen. It's the individual who can bring a tear to our eyes and cause us to take pen in hand. It is the individual who has acted or tried to act who will not only force a decision, but have a hand in shaping it. Whether the individual acts in the legal, governmental, or private realm, one concerned and dedicated person can meaningfully affect what some say is an uncaring world.

So be a full participant in life's opportunities. Aim high. If you strive for excellence you can and should have a substantial impact on the world in which you live.

RUTH BADER GINSBURG, ASSOCIATE JUSTICE OF THE U. S. SUPREME COURT

Be A Little Deaf

Sometimes people say unkind or thoughtless things, and when they do, it is best to be a little hard of hearing – to tune out and not snap back in anger or impatience. Anger, resentment, envy, and self-pity are wasteful reactions. They greatly drain one's time. They sap energy better devoted to productive endeavors. Of course it is important to be a good listener – to pay attention to teachers, coworkers, and spouses. But is also pays, sometimes, to be a little deaf.

RUTH BADER GINSBURG

★

SUSAN COLLINS
UNITED STATES SENATOR, MAINE

Read To Your Children

"I cannot live without books," Thomas Jefferson once said, and his enthusiasm was hardly overstated. I share President Jefferson's love of a good book and a comfortable stretch of time in which to read it. But reading is also a pleasure that has to be cultivated, and it is vital for parents to expose their children to books at an early age. Taking just 30 minutes a day to read to children is not only a worthwhile investment but also a wonderful experience.

SUSAN COLLINS

Children whose parents read to them three or more times a week are almost twice as likely to be able to identify every letter of the alphabet. They are also more likely to be able to count to 20, write their own names, and read or pretend to read. When a child enters kindergarten already recognizing letters and familiar with books, she or he is better prepared to learn and less likely to encounter difficulty in learning to read.

Capturing the spirit of the day can be done through one simple act: provide a loving lap for a child and spend some time opening his or her world through a book. I applaud all schoolteachers, librarians, and most of all, our parents, for their commitment to teaching America's children the joys of reading.

11

★

MAYA ANGELOU
AUTHOR, TEACHER, POET
Internalize Success

Money is very important and should not be denied or scorned. It's very important. It is not, however, a measure of success. Success is always internal, but what money does is afford the person who has it the chance to be generous to herself and others.

MAYA ANGELOU

Success is internal, being able to look in the mirror when you brush your teeth and like what you see, and not drop your eyes. Liking yourself, and liking the person you want to be and liking the person you're trying to become. And that is it. That puts you at ease in any company. Whether you're black in white company, or white in black company, you're at ease. Christian with Jews at ease, because you know your heart and you know how you feel. That is true success.

★

Elizabeth Dole
U. S. Senator, North Carolina

Be The Messenger

God's gift to all of his children is liberty – and also justice and equality, tolerance and opportunity. These belong to all people – no matter where they live. Our free society and global economy require an environment that respects liberty and individual rights.

Elizabeth Dole

The road ahead beckons. It leads to a world of limitless possibility. Travel as much as you can. Engage your fellow man, globally. Work to understand other cultures. And, above all, listen. You are our messengers. To those abroad, show them that we have no sinister motives, share with them our ideals of freedom and tolerance. Show them that we only wish to share freedom and liberty with all of mankind.

Within your chest beats the most powerful antidote to despair that the world has ever known. When you find the sense of mission that summons you to selflessness, you will find the contribution only you can make to life. And no pain or suffering, no affliction or challenge can stand against the combined hearts of people committed to action. One individual can make a world of difference, even a different world.

★

QUEEN NOOR
JORDAN

Form Coalitions For Peace

There are infinite ways that together we can contribute to coalitions to create a more stable, secure and equitable world. We live in a time when it is critically important to build such coalitions. My late husband, King Hussein, believed that peace resides ultimately not in the hands of governments, but in the hands of people. He said that real victories are those that protect human life, not those that result from its destruction or emerge from its ashes.

QUEEN NOOR

Education is the single most effective tool in our peace arsenal. It can provide techniques for resolving differences without conflict, broader perspectives for looking at the world from others' points of view, and the resources, skills and new thinking that are the currency of the global information economy. Successful coalitions cannot be simply temporary alliances of like-minded nations, determined to achieve their own ends. They need to encompass a wealth of enduring, committed partnerships - among governments, business, and civil society, and above all among all kinds of people.

You can add your voice to the many other voices around the world calling for peace, justice and tolerance. Thanks to the power of technology in the service of democratic principles never before in human history have ordinary people had so much opportunity to do good.

Yes, now, more than ever, is the time for true coalitions - for webs, for networks of people reaching out to each other. If we break down the walls of misperception and mistrust, we will achieve our radically new definition of security - not a fortress for the few, but a safety net for all.

KAY BAILEY HUTCHISON
U. S. SENATOR, TEXAS

Follow These Rules To Success

Paying attention to detail pays off - "Sweat the small stuff. If it's worth doing, it's worth becoming an expert at it. And experts are always in demand."

KAY BAILEY HUTCHISON

Don't compromise your principles - "These are cynical times. There's a sense that it's OK to cut corners, that everything is relative and negotiable. Not so. Honor and truth remain cherished principles because only they work in the long-run."

Remember your friends and alma mater - "Friends found in college can help you stay grounded amidst life's ups and downs."

Breathe life into the American dream by not fearing failure - "Failure stops only those who choose to stop. Learn from failure, drive on and your successes will enrich your life and the American dream."

★

DR. MARGARET MARY FITZPATRICK, S.C., COLLEGE PRESIDENT

Observe Your Actions

A principle that I learned a while ago in philosophy class is, "Action follows being." The perennial quest for understanding "who I am" can be answered very easily by observing one's actions. I wonder, "How would someone describe me after observing me for a week?" Would anyone know that I am a good person after watching my footsteps?"

MARGARET MARY FITZPATRICK

The fundamental commandment to "love God and one's neighbor" has to lead us in our decision-making each day. Whether it is how we are using the earth's resources, how we care for children and the elderly, or how we define who is our neighbor, in these actions we are defining ourselves.

Being proactive and reflectively open to opportunities are two important stances in this journey of becoming our best. Being our best, we honor our parents and teachers as we, in turn, have a positive impact on those we touch.

We are each uniquely beautiful and gifted. To be our best selves is such a great gift to the world.

Watch out world, here I come!

1.

Instead of looking at life as a narrowing funnel, we can see it ever widening to choose the things we want to do, to take the wisdoms we've learned and create something.

Liz Carpenter, Writer

2.

The penalty for success is to be bored by the people who used to snub you.

Lady Nancy Astor,
First Woman in House of Commons

3.

You don't manage people; you manage things. You lead people.

Grace Hooper, Admiral

4.

If you always do what interests you, at least one person is pleased.

Katharine Hepburn, Actor

5.

God does not ask your ability or your inability. He asks only your availability.

Mary Kay Ash, Entrepreneur

6.

In the first grade, I already knew the pattern of my life. I didn't know the living of it, but I knew the line … From the first day in school until the day I graduated, everyone gave me one hundred plus in art. Well, where do you go in life? You go to the place where you got one hundred plus.

Louise Nevelson, Artist

7.

Most of us who aspire to be tops in our fields don't really consider the amount of work required to stay tops.

Althea Gibson, Tennis Player

8.

Don't be humble; you're not that great.

Golda Meir, Prime Minister

9.

It's not the load that breaks you down, it's the way you carry it.

Lena Horne, Singer

10.

Accomplishments have no color.

Leontyne Price, Opera Singer

11.

When I stand before God at the end of my life, I would hope that I would not have a single bit of talent left and could say, "I used everything you gave me."

Erma Bombeck, Writer

12.

We may encounter many defeats but we must not be defeated.

Maya Angelou, Writer

13.

Fear is a disease that eats away at logic and makes man inhuman.

Marian Anderson, Opera Singer

14.

It will never rain roses: when we want to have more roses we must plant more trees.

George Eliot, Writer

15.

I'm really glad that your young people missed the Depression and missed the big war. But I do regret that they missed the leaders that I knew, leaders who told us when things were tough and that we'd have to sacrifice, and that these difficulties might last awhile... They brought us together and they gave us a sense of national purpose.

Ann Richards, Politician

16.

What really matters is what you do with what you have.

Shirley Lord, Writer

17.

A champion is afraid of losing. Everyone else is afraid of winning.

Billie Jean King, Tennis Player

18.

Failure is impossible.

Susan B. Anthony, Women's Rights Activist

19.

I think one's feelings waste themselves in words; they ought all to be distilled into actions which bring results.

Florence Nightingale, Nurse

20.

Mr. Meant-to has a friend, his name is Didn't-Do. Have you met them? They live together in a house called Never-Win. And I am told that it is haunted by the Ghost of Might-have-Been.

Marva Collins, Educator

21.

No person has the right to rain on your dreams.

Marian Wright Edelman, Educator

22.

Not being beautiful was the true blessing...Not being beautiful forced me to develop my inner resources. The pretty girl has a handicap to overcome.

Golda Meir, Prime Minister

23.

If you want to accomplish the goals of your life, you have to begin with the spirit.

Oprah Winfrey, Talk Show Host

24.

I long to accomplish a great and noble task, but it is my chief duty to accomplish small tasks as if they were great and noble.

Helen Keller, Writer

25.

You don't make progress by standing on the sidelines, whimpering and complaining. You make progress by implementing ideas.

Shirley Chisholm, Congresswoman

26.

Think of all the beauty still left around you and be happy.

Anne Frank, Writer

27.

My passions were all gathered together like fingers that made a fist. Drive is considered aggression today; I knew it then as purpose.

Bette Davis, Actor

28.

Although I may not be a lioness, I am a lion's cub, and inherit many of his qualities; and as long as the King of France treats me gently he will find me as gentle and tractable as he can desire; but if he be rough, I shall take the trouble to be just as troublesome and offensive to him as I can.

Queen Elizabeth I

29.

You have to accept whatever comes and the only important thing is that you meet it with the best you have to give.

Eleanor Roosevelt, First Lady

30.

You can't turn back the clock. But you can wind it up again.

Bonnie Prudden, Fitness pioneer.

31.

There is a growing strength in women, but it's in the forehead, not in the forearm.

Beverly Sills, Opera Singer

32.

Fashions in bigotry come and go. The right thing lasts.

Mary Hays, Writer

33.

I learned the value of hard work by working hard.

Dr. Margaret Mary Fitzpatrick, S.C., College President

34.

Contrary to popular opinion, the hustle is not a new dance step—it is an old business procedure.

Fran Lebowitz, Writer

35.

One only gets to the top rung of the ladder by steadily climbing up one at a time, and suddenly all sorts of powers, all sorts of abilities which you thought never belonged to you—suddenly become within your own possibility and you think, "Well, I'll have a go, too."

Margaret Thatcher, Prime Minister

36.

I wanted to be scared again...I wanted to feel unsure again. That's the only way I learn, the only way I feel challenged.

Connie Chung, Reporter

37.

Life itself is the proper binge.

Julia Child, Chef

38.

To be tested is good. The challenged life
may be the best therapist.

Gail Sheehy, Writer

39.

How very little can be done under the
spirit of fear.

Florence Nightingale, Nurse

40.

Success is important only to the extent
that it puts one in a position to do more
things one likes to do.

Sarah Caldwell, Conductor

41.

Beauty can't amuse you, but brainwork—
reading, writing, thinking—can.

Helen Gurley Brown, Publisher

42.

When people keep telling you that you can't do a thing, you kind of like to try it.

Margaret Chase Smith, Senator

43.

There is no such thing as security. There never has been.

Germaine Greer, Writer

44.

To follow without halt, one aim; there is the secret of success. And success? What is it? I do not fnd it in the applause of the theater, it lies rather in the satisfaction of accomplishment.

Anna Pavlova, Ballerina

45.

Become so wrapped up in something that you forget to be afraid.

Lady Bird Johnson, First Lady

46.

People see God every day; they just
don't recognize Him.

Pearl Bailey, Singer

47.

I don't wait for moods. You accomplish
nothing if you do that. Your mind must
know it has got to get down to earth.

Pearl S. Buck, Writer

48.

Character cannot be developed in ease
and quiet. Only through experiences of
trial and suffering can the soul be
strengthened, vision cleared, ambition
inspired and success achieved.

Helen Keller, Writer

49.

Mistakes are part of the dues one pays
for a full life.

Sophia Loren, Actor

50.

No one has it who isn't capable of genuinely liking others, at least at the actual moment of meeting and speaking. Charm is always genuine; it may be superficial but it isn't false.

P.D. James, Writer

51.

I look forward to being older, when what you look like becomes less and less an issue and what you are is the point.

Susan Sarandon, Actor

52.

Moral cowardice that keeps us from speaking our minds is as dangerous to this country as irresponsible talk. The right way is not always the popular and easy way. Standing for right when it is unpopular is a true test of moral character.

Senator Margaret Chase Smith

53.

On my underground railroad I never ran my train off the track. And I never lost a passenger.

Harriet Tubman, Conductor,
Underground Railroad

54.

Fear drives you and makes you better.

Donna E. Shalala, President, Univ. of Miami

55.

One never notices what has been done; one can only see what remains to be done.

Marie Curie, Physicist

56.

We are not interested in the possibilities of defeat.

Queen Victoria

57.

Life is what we make it, always has been, always will be.

Grandma Moses, Painter

58.

The most important thing about motivation is goal setting. You should always have a goal.

Francie Larrieu Smith, Olympian

59.

Yesterday I dared to struggle.

Today I dare to win.

Bernadette Devlin, Social Activist

60.

Science may have found a cure for most evils; but it has found no remedy for the worst of them all – the apathy of human beings.

Helen Keller, Writer

61.

No great deed is done by falterers who ask for certainty.

George Eliot, Writer

62.

Don't agonize. Organize.

Florynce Kennedy, Lawyer

63.

No matter how big or soft or warm your bed is, you still have to get out of it.

Grace Slick, Singer

64.

My great hope is to laugh as much as I cry; to get my work done and try to love somebody and have the courage to accept the love in return.

Maya Angelou, Writer

65.

I'm in love with the potential of miracles.
For me, the safest place is out on a limb.

Shirley MacLaine, Actor

66.

Nothing's far when one wants
to get there.

Queen Marie

67.

The problem with beauty is that it's like
being born rich and getting poorer.

Joan Collins, Actor

68.

Many older women are inhibited and
afraid to act. It is such a waste of human
potential.

Frances Lear, Publisher

69.

The bitterest tears shed over graves are for words left unsaid and deeds left undone.

Harriet Beecher Stowe, Author

70.

You know, your career is your career. Your life is your life!

Sissy Spacek, Actor

71.

I am not afraid … I was born to do this.

Saint Joan of Arc

72.

Success is having a flair for the thing that you are doing; knowing that is not enough, that you have got to have hard work and a certain sense of purpose.

Margaret Thatcher, Prime Minister

73.

I have always had a dread of becoming a passenger in life.

Queen Margreth II

74.

Your real security is yourself. You know you can do it, and they can't ever take that away from you.

Mae West, Actor

75.

Success is counted sweetest by those who ne'er succeed.

Emily Dickinson, Poet

76.

Trouble is a part of your life, and if you don't share it you don't give the person who loves you enough chance to love you enough.

Dinah Shore, Singer

77.

The secret of joy in work is contained in one word—excellence. To know how to do something well is to enjoy it.

Pearl S. Buck, Writer

78.

Success is a state of mind. If you want success, start thinking of yourself as a success.

Dr. Joyce Brothers, Psychologist

79.

The greatest part of our happiness depends on our dispositions, not our circumstances.

Martha Washington, First Lady

80.

Excellence is not an act but a habit. The things you do the most are the things you will do best.

Marva Collins, Educator

81.

Just go out there and do what you've
got to do.

Martina Navratilova, Tennis Player

82.

The real power behind whatever success
I have now was something I found within
myself-something that's in all of us, I
think, a little piece of God just waiting to
be discovered.

Tina Turner, Singer

83.

Women share with men the need for
personal success, even the taste for
power, and no longer are we willing to
satisfy those needs through the
achievements of surrogates, whether
husbands, children or merely role models.

Senator Elizabeth Dole

84.

What I cannot love, I overlook.

Anais Nin, Writer

85.

No one can build her security upon the nobleness of another person.

Willa Cather, Writer

86.

Love is a fruit in the season at all times, and within reach of every hand.

Mother Teresa, Humanitarian

87.

And as we let our own light shine, we unconsciously give other people permission to do the same. As we are liberated from our fear, our presence automatically liberates others.

Marianne Williamson, Author

88.

Failure is just another way to learn how to do something right.

Marian Wright Edelman, Educator

89.

I said to myself, "I'll paint what I see." What the flower is to me but I'll paint it big and they will be surprised into taking time to look at it.

Georgia O'Keefe, Artist

90.

For me, life is all about growth.

Janet Jackson, Singer

91.

One of the things I learned the hard way was that it doesn't pay to get discouraged. Keeping busy and making optimism a way of life can restore your faith in yourself.

Lucille Ball, Comedian

92.

Life is a succession of moments. To live
each one is to succeed.

Corita Kent, Graphic Artist

93.

Slaying the dragon of delay is no sport
for the short-winded.

Sandra Day O'Connor, Supreme Court Justice

94.

It is the mind that makes the body.

Sojourner Truth, Women's Rights Activist

95.

A woman is like a teabag –
you can't tell how strong she is until
you put her in hot water.

Nancy Reagan, First Lady

96.

Failure must be but a challenge to others.

Amelia Earhart, Pilot

97.

I don't think black or white. I have to tell
you that. I think of human beings,
people ... My mother raised me that way.

Sarah Vaughan, Singer

98.

I think success has no rules, but you can
learn a lot from failure.

Jean Kerr, Playwright

99.

He who devotes sixteen hours a day to
hard study may become at sixty as wise
as he thought himself at twenty.

Mary Wilson Little, Author

100.

I don't think about risks much. I just do what I want to do. If you gotta go, you gotta go.

Lillian Carter, Nurse

101.

Although the world is full of suffering, it is full also of the overcoming of it.

Helen Keller, Writer

102.

The richest man in the world is not the one who still has the first dollar he ever earned. It's the man who still has his best friend.

Martha Mason, Actor

103.

Life appears to me too short to be spent in nursing animosity or registering wrong.

Charlotte Bronte, Writer

104.

Perhaps it is impossible for a person who does no good not to do harm.

Harriet Beecher Stowe, Writer

105.

Determination and perseverance move the world; thinking that others will do it for you is a sure way to fail.

Marva Collins, Educator

106.

When you come right down to it, the secret of having it all is loving it all.

Dr. Joyce Brothers, Psychologist

107.

I compensate for big risks by always doing my homework and being well-prepared. I can take on larger risks by reducing the overall risk.

Donna E. Shalala, President, University of Miami

108.

I was brought up to believe that the only thing worth doing was to add to the sum of accurate information in this world.

Margaret Mead, Anthropologist

109.

False values begin with the worship of things.

Susan Sontag, Writer

110.

When you do nothing, you feel overwhelmed and powerless. But when you get involved, you feel the sense of hope and accomplishment that comes from knowing you are working to make things better.

Pauline R. Kezer, Politician

111.

I am treating you as my friend, asking you to share my present minuses in the hope that I can ask you to share my future pluses.

Katherine Mansfield, Writer

112.

All things are possible until they are proved impossible—even the impossible may only be so, as of now.

Pearl S. Buck, Writer

113.

Adventure is worthwhile in itself.

Amelia Earhart, Pilot

114.

Happiness is not a possession to be prized, it is a quality of thought, a state of mind.

Daphne du Maurier, Writer

115.

Winning the prize wasn't half as exciting as doing the work itself.

Maria Goeppert Mayer, Nobel Prize winner.

116.

Integrity is so perishable in the summer months of success.

Vanessa Redgrave, Actor

117.

I found, while thinking about the far-reaching world of the creative black woman, that often the truest answer to a question that really matters can be found very close.

Alice Walker, Writer

118.

You've got to take the initiative and play your game ... confidence makes the difference.

Chris Evert, Tennis Player

119.

A life of reaction is a life of slavery, intellectually and spiritually. One must fight for a life of action, not reaction.

Rita Mae Brown, Writer

120.

One of the pleasantest things those of us who write or paint do is to have the daily miracle. It does come.

Gertrude Stein, Writer

121.

In spite of everything I still believe that people are really good at heart.

Anne Frank, Writer

122.

You can eat an elephant one bite at a time.

Mary Kay Ash, Entrepreneur

123.

The mere sense of living is joy enough.

Emily Dickinson, Poet

124.

Success is a public affair.
Failure is a private funeral.

Rosalind Russell, Actor

125.

Power ... is not an end in itself,
but is an instrument that must be used
toward an end.

Jeane J. Kirkpatrick, Ambassador

126.

You cannot shake hands with a
clenched fist.

Indira Gandhi, Prime Minister

127.

I believe in the soul. Furthermore, I believe it is prompt accountability for one's choices, a willing acceptance of responsibility for one's thoughts, behavior, and actions that makes it powerful.

Alice Walker, Writer

128.

Do not call for black power or green power. Call for brain power.

Barbara Jordan, Congresswoman

129.

My will shall shape the future. Whether I fail or succeed shall be no man's doing but my own. I am the force; I can clear any obstacle before me or I can be lost in the maze. My choice; my responsibility; win or lose, only I hold the key to my destiny.

Elaine Maxwell, Lawyer

130.

Risk! Risk anything! Care no more for the opinions of others, for those voices. Do the hardest thing on earth for you. Act for yourself. Face the truth.

Katherine Mansfield, Writer

131.

I was determined to achieve the total freedom that our history lessons taught us we were entitled to, no matter what the sacrifice.

Rosa Parks, Civil Rights Activist

132.

I can feel the wind go by when I run. It feels good. It feels fast.

Evelyn Ashford, Olympian

133.

I'm five-feet-four, but I always feel six-foot-one, tall and strong.

Yvette Mimieux, Actor

134.

Good habits can be fine things. If you say your prayers every night there comes a time when they grow more meaningful to you.

Marian Anderson, Opera Singer

135.

Opportunities are usually disguised as hard work, so most people don't recognize them.

Ann Landers, Writer

136.

She lacks confidence, she craves admiration insatiably. She lives on the reflections of herself in the eyes of others. She does not dare to be herself.

Anais Nin, Writer

137.

A single hand's turn given heartily to the world's great work helps one amazingly with one's own small tasks.

Louisa M. Alcott, Writer

138.

It takes a lot of courage to show your dreams to someone else.

Erma Bombeck, Writer

139.

You can't get spoiled if you do your own ironing.

Meryl Streep, Actor

140.

Let us always meet each other with a smile, for the smile is the beginning of love.

Mother Teresa, Humanitarian

141.

If I have to, I can do anything. I am strong, I am invincible, I am Woman.

Helen Reddy, Singer

142.

The stubbornness I had as a child has been transmitted into perseverance. I can let go but I don't give up. I don't beat myself up about negative things.

Phylicia Rashad, Actor

143.

The only causes of regret are laziness, outbursts of temper, hurting others, prejudice, jealousy and envy.

Germaine Greer, Writer

144.

You have to be taught to be second class; you're not born that way.

Lena Horne, Singer

145.

I have met brave women who are exploring the outer edge of human possibility, with no history to guide them, and with a courage to make themselves vulnerable that I find moving beyond words.

Gloria Steinem, Writer

146.

To tend, unfailingly, unflinchingly, towards a goal, is the secret of success.

Anna Pavlova, Ballerina

147.

The main dangers in this life are the people who want to change everything ... or nothing.

Lady Nancy Astor, Politician

148.

There's no deodorant like success.

Elizabeth Taylor, Actor

149.

I do not know anyone who has got to the top without hard work. That is the recipe. It will not always get you to the top, but it should get you pretty near.

Margaret Thatcher, Prime Minister

150.

You can have anything you want if you want it desperately enough. You must want it with an inner exuberance that erupts through the skin and joins the energy that created the world.

Sheila Graham, Journalist

151.

Education remains the key to both economic and political empowerment.

Barbara Jordan, Congresswoman

152.

Success supposes endeavor.

Jane Austen, Writer

153.

Courage, it would seem, is nothing less than the power to overcome danger, misfortune, fear, injustice, while continuing to affirm inwardly that life with all its sorrows is good; that everything is meaningful even if in a sense beyond our understanding; and that there is always tomorrow.

Dorothy Thompson, Journalist

154.

It takes as much courage to have tried and failed as it does to have tried and succeeded.

Anne Morrow Lindbergh, Writer

155.

I have never wanted to be anything but a gymnast. Maybe it is dangerous – but when you start thinking of danger, you might as well give up.

Olga Korbut, Olympian

156.

Study as if you are going to live forever;
live as if you were going to die tomorrow.

Marion Mitchell, Educator

157.

I personally measure success in terms of
the contributions an individual makes to
her or his fellow human beings.

Margaret Mead, Anthropologist

158.

The challenges of change are always
hard. It is important that we begin to
unpack those challenges that confront this
nation and realize that we each have a
role that requires us to change and
become more responsible for shaping our
own future.

Senator Hillary Rodham Clinton

159.

Generally speaking, we are all happier when we are still striving for achievement than when the prize is in our hands.

Margot Fonteyn, Ballerina

160.

Success in show business depends on your ability to make and keep friends.

Sophie Tucker, Singer

161.

Any coward can fight a battle when he's sure of winning.

George Eliot, Writer

162.

The human race does command its own destiny and that destiny can eventually embrace the stars.

Lorraine Hansberry, Playwright

163.

The way I see it, if you want the rainbow, you gotta put up with the rain.

Dolly Parton, Singer

164.

No person is your friend (or kin) who demands your silence, or denies your right to grow and be perceived as fully blossomed as you were intended.

Alice Walker, Writer

165.

I realized that if what we call human nature can be changed, then absolutely anything is possible. And from that moment, my life changed.

Shirley MacLaine, Actor

166.

There is no sin punished more implacably by nature than the sin of resistance to change.

Anne Morrow Lindbergh, Writer

167.

Character contributes to beauty. It fortifies a woman as her youth fades. A mode of conduct, a standard of courage, discipline, fortitude, and integrity can do a great deal to make a woman beautiful.

Jacqueline Bisset, Actor

168.

You must learn day by day, year by year, to broaden your horizon. The more things you love, the more you are interested in, the more you enjoy, the more you are indignant about, the more you have left when anything happens.

Ethel Barrymore, Actor

169.

To achieve, you need thought. You have to know what you are doing and that's real power.

Ayn Rand, Writer

170.

People complain all the time about how busy they are, but there is time enough for all the things that a person really wants to do. When I was working, I got only three or four hours of sleep each night. Sometimes I worked straight through for two or three days. I had goals I was working toward. That motivated me and I was able to push hard.

Oseola McCarty, Philanthropist

171.

I always had something to shoot for each year: to jump one inch farther.

Jackie Joyner Kersee, Olympian

172.

We never know how high we are
Till we are called to rise;
And then, if we are true to plan,
Our statures touch the skies.

Emily Dickinson, Poet

173.

The challenge is to practice politics as the
art of making what appears to be
impossible, possible.

Senator Hillary Rodham Clinton

174.

In order to be irreplaceable one must
always be different.

Coco Chanel, Fashion Designer

175.

Be Black, shine, aim high.

Leontyne Price, Opera Singer

176.

Without discipline, there is no life at all.

Katharine Hepburn, Actor

177.

If particular care and attention is not paid to the ladies, we are determined to foment a rebellion, and will not hold ourselves bound by any laws in which we have no voice or representation.

Abigail Adams, First Lady

178.

To have that sense of one's intrinsic worth which constitutes self-respect is potentially to have everything.

Joan Didion, Writer

179.

Whoever said, "It's not whether you win or lose that counts," probably lost.

Martina Navratilova, Tennis Player

180.

Begin somewhere; you cannot build a reputation on what you intend to do.

Liz Smith, Writer

181.

I very sinearly [sic] wish you would exert yourself so as to keep all your matters in order your self without depending on others as that is the only way to be happy to have all your business in your own hands.

Martha Washington, First Lady

182.

Young people should find something they're good at. They need to practice to build skills and to keep their minds busy. I think working hard gives them an important feeling of accomplishment.

Oseola McCarty, Philanthropist

183.

I pray hard, work hard and leave the rest to God.

Florence Griffith Joyner, Olympian

184.

The one who cares the most wins … That's how I knew I'd end up with everyone else waving the white flags and not me. That's how I knew I'd be the last person standing when it was all over … I cared the most.

Roseanne Arnold, Actor

185.

My ability to survive personal crises is really a mark of the character of my people. Individually and collectively, we react with a tenacity that allows us again and again to bounce back from adversity.

Chief Wilma Mankiller, Cherokee Chief

186.

It is best to act with confidence, no matter how little right you have to it.

Lillian Hellman, Playwright

187.

The greatest gift is not being afraid to question.

Ruby Dee, Actor

188.

Our deeds determine us, as much as we determine our deeds.

George Eliot, Writer

189.

Winning may not be everything, but losing has little to recommend it.

Dianne Feinstein, Senator

190.

Yesterday I dared to struggle. Today I dare to win.

Bernadette Devlin, Social activist

191.

To find joy in work is to discover the fountain of youth.

Pearl S. Buck, Writer

192.

I must govern the clock, not be governed by it.

Golda Meir, Prime Minister

193.

Because I am a woman, I must make unusual efforts to succeed. If I fail, no one will say, "She doesn't have what it takes." They will say, "Women don't have what it takes."

Clare Boothe Luce, Journalist

194.

Always aim for achievement, and forget
about success.

Helen Hayes, Actor

195.

I believe in hard work. It keeps the
wrinkles out of the mind and the spirit.

Helena Rubinstein, Entrepreneur

196.

To love what you do and feel that it
matters—how could anything be
more fun?

Katharine Graham, Publisher

197.

Some people regard discipline as a
chore. For me, it is a kind of order that
sets me free to fly.

Julie Andrews, Actor

198.

I suppose I could have stayed home, baked cookies and had teas. The work that I have done ... has been aimed ... to assure that women can make the choices ... whether it's full-time career, full-time motherhood or some combination.

Senator Hillary Rodham Clinton

199.

I believe in my work and the joy of it. You have to be with the work and the work has to be with you. It absorbs you totally and you absorb it totally. Everything must fall by the wayside by comparison.

Louise Nevelson, Artist

200.

There are no shortcuts to any place worth going.

Beverly Sills, Opera Singer

201.

The big gap between the ability of actors is confidence.

Kathleen Turner, Actor

202.

I am so full of my work, I can't stop to eat or sleep, or for anything but a daily run.

Louisa May Alcott, Writer

203.

At the end of your life, you will never regret not having passed one more test, not winning one more verdict or not closing one more deal. You will regret time not spent with a husband, a friend, a child or a parent.

Barbara Bush, First Lady

204.

If you don't look out for others, who will look out for you?

Whoopi Goldberg, Actor

205.

To have meaningful work is a
tremendous happiness.

Rita Mae Brown, Writer

206.

There can be no substitute for work,
neither affection nor physical well-being
can replace it.

Maria Montessori, Educator

207.

One is happy as a result of one's own
efforts—once one knows the necessary
ingredients of happiness—simple tastes, a
certain degree of courage, self-denial to a
point, love of work, and, above all,
a clear conscience.

George Sand, Writer

208.

My satisfaction comes from my commitment to advancing a better world.

Faye Wattleton, Health Activist

209.

Supposing you have tried and failed again and again. You may have a fresh start any moment you choose, for this thing that we call "failure" is not the falling down, but the staying down.

Mary Pickford, Actor

210.

There is no time for cut-and-dried monotony. There is time for work. And time for love. That leaves no other time.

Coco Chanel, Fashion Designer

211.

People are not the best because they work hard. They work hard because they are the best.

Bette Midler, Actor

212.

Striving for excellence motivates you; striving for perfection is demoralizing.

Dr. Harriet Braiker, Psychologist

213.

I may be compelled to face danger, but never fear it, and while our soldiers can stand and fight, I can stand and feed and nurse them.

Clara Barton, Founder, American Red Cross

214.

The ladder of success is best climbed by stepping on the rungs of opportunity.

Ayn Rand, Author

215.

Optimism is the faith that leads to achievement. Nothing can be done without hope and confidence.

Helen Keller, Writer

216.

If you rest, you rust.

Helen Hayes, Actor

217.

I have no regrets. I wouldn't have lived my life the way I did if I was going to worry about what people were going to say.

Ingrid Bergman, Actor

218.

The only safe ship in a storm is leadership.

Faye Wattleton, Health Activist

219.

You don't just luck into things … You build step by step, whether it's friendships or opportunities.

Barbara Bush, First Lady

220.

The willingness to accept responsibility for one's own life is the source from which self-respect springs.

Joan Didion, Writer

221.

Always be smarter than the people who hire you.

Lena Horne, Singer

222.

So many women just don't know how great they really are. They come to us all vogue outside and vague on the inside.

Mary Kay Ash, Entrepreneur

223.

I always thought I should be treated
like a star.

Madonna, Singer

224.

Readers are leaders. Thinkers succeed.

Marva Collins, Educator

225.

Nothing in life is to be feared.
It is only to be understood.

Marie Curie, Physicist

226.

I can remember walking as a child. It was
not customary to say you were fatigued.
It was customary to complete the goal of
the expedition.

Katharine Hepburn, Actor

227.

I finally figured out the only reason to be alive is to enjoy it.

Rita Mae Brown, Writer

228.

Invest in the human soul. Who knows, it might be a diamond in the rough.

Mary McLeod Bethune, Educator

229.

The only people with whom you should try to get even, are those who have helped you.

May Maloo, Writer

230.

Luck is not chance, it's toil; fortune's expensive smile is earned.

Emily Dickinson, Poet

231.

I always regarded myself as the pillar
of my life.

Meryl Streep, Actor

232.

Education is a loan to be repaid
with gift of self.

Lady Bird Johnson, First Lady

233.

I never intended to become a run-of-the-
mill person.

Barbara Jordan, Congresswoman

234.

Wherever I have knocked, a door has
opened. Wherever I have wandered, a path
has appeared. I have been helped, supported,
encouraged, and nurtured by people of all
races, creeds, colors, and dreams.

Alice Walker, Writer

235.

For a long time the only time I felt beautiful—in the sense of being complete as a woman, as a human being—was when I was singing.

Leontyne Price, Opera Singer

236.

Love is a choice you make from moment to moment.

Dr. Barbara De Angelis, Psychologist

237.

It is easier to live through someone else than to become complete yourself.

Betty Friedan, Feminist

238.

I am where I am because I believe in all possibilities.

Whoopi Goldberg, Actor

239.

The one important thing I have learned over the years is the difference between taking one's work seriously, and taking one's self seriously. The first is imperative, and the second is disastrous.

Margot Fonteyn, Ballerina

240.

Only you can know how much you can give to every aspect of your life. Try to decide what is the most important. And if you do, then only occasionally will you resent or regret the demands of the marriage, the career, or the child, or the staying.

Barbara Walters, Journalist

241.

There is a way to look at the past. Don't hide from it. It will not catch you—if you don't repeat it.

Pearl Bailey, Singer

242.

I am not afraid of storms, for I am learning how to sail my ship.

Louisa May Alcott, Writer

243.

The process of empowerment cannot be simplistically defined in accordance with our own particular class interests. We must learn to lift as we climb.

Angela Davis, Activist

244.

Think wrongly, if you please, but in all cases think for yourself.

Doris Lessing, Writer

245.

Are we willing to give up some things we like to do, to move on to those things we must do?

Satenig St. Marie, Writer

246.

Courage is the price that life exacts for granting peace. The soul that knows it not, knows no release from little things; knows not the livid loneliness of fear.

Amelia Earhart, Pilot

247.

You just have to learn not to care about the dust mites under the beds.

Margaret Mead, Anthropologist

248.

Sometimes I worry about being a success in a mediocre world.

Lily Tomlin, Comedian

249.

I believe you are your work. Don't trade the very stuff of your life, time, for nothing more than dollars. That's a rotten bargain.

Rita Mae Brown, Writer

250.

It is true that in crucial situations, I have lost matches. But I knew I was giving 110 percent.

Zina Garrison, Tennis Player

251.

Accept that all of us can be hurt, that all of us can – and surely will at times – fail. Other vulnerabilities, like being embarrassed or risking love, can be terrifying, too. I think we should follow a simple rule: if we can take the worst, take the risk.

Dr. Joyce Brothers, Psychologist

252.

Imagination is the highest kite one can fly.

Lauren Bacall, Actor

253.

Let me listen to me and not to them.

Gertrude Stein, Writer

254.

Only yourself can heal you,
Only yourself can lead you.

Sara Teasdale, Poet

255.

You need to hold the highest, grandest
vision for yourself and it can be done.
When you allow yourself to be the best,
the best follows you.

Oprah Winfrey, Talk Show Host

256.

You can't be brave if you've only had
wonderful things happen to you.

Mary Tyler Moore, Actor

257.

Take your work seriously, but never yourself.

Margot Fonteyn, Dancer

258.

There are people who put their dreams in a little box and say, "Yes, I've got dreams, of course, I've got dreams." Then they put the box away and bring it out once in awhile to look in it, and yep, they're still there. These are great dreams, but they never even get out of the box. It takes an uncommon amount of guts to put your dreams on the line, to hold them up and say, "How good or how bad am I?" That's where the courage comes in.

Erma Bombeck, Writer

259.

If I have a philosophy of life, it's about making your own way. Going out and getting it done. Not expecting it to be done for you.

Janet Jackson, Singer

260.

The way of progress is neither
swift nor easy.

Marie Curie, Physicist

261.

I have always been driven by some
distant music—a battle hymn no doubt—
for I have been at war from the
beginning. I've never looked back before.
I've never had the time and it has always
seemed so dangerous. To look back is to
relax one's vigil.

Bette Davis, Actor

262.

There is no other solution to man's
progress but the day's honest work, the
day's honest decisions, the day's generous
utterances and the day's good deed.

Clare Boothe Luce, Diplomat

263.

Many women have more power than they recognize, and they're very hesitant to use it, for they fear they won't be loved.

Patricia Schroeder, Congresswoman

264.

All adventures, especially into new territory, are scary.

Sally Ride, Astronaut

265.

Light tomorrow with today.

Elizabeth Barrett Browning, Poet

266.

I would rather die a meaningful death than to live a meaningless life.

Corazon Aquino, Politician

267.

It takes steady nerves and being a fighter
to stay out there.

Wilma Rudolph, Olympian

268.

… I am perfectly willing to expose a
great deal of my foolishness because I
don't think that infallibility is anything to
be proud of. I don't believe that I should
be perfect.

Nikki Giovanni, Poet

269.

As long as one keeps searching, the
answers come.

Joan Baez, Singer

270.

You never find yourself until you
face the truth.

Pearl Bailey, Singer

271.

I've never sought success in order to get fame and money; it's the talent and the passion that count in success.

Ingrid Bergman, Actor

272.

Everyone thought I was bold and fearless and even arrogant, but inside I was always quaking.

Katharine Hepburn, Actor

273.

You gain strength, courage and confidence by every experience in which you really stop to look fear in the face … You must do the thing which you think you cannot do.

Eleanor Roosevelt, First Lady

274.

You must learn day by day, year by year, to broaden your horizon. The more things you love, the more you are interested in, the more you enjoy, the more you are indignant about, the more you have left when anything happens.

Ethel Barrymore, Actor

275.

You have to count on living every single day in a way you believe will make you feel good about your life—so that if it were over tomorrow, you'd be content with yourself.

Jane Seymour, Actor

276.

It's fun to get together and have something good to eat at least once a day. That's what human life is all about— enjoying things.

Julia Child, Chef

277.

It is capitalist America that produced the modern independent woman. Never in history have women had more freedom of choice in regard to dress, behavior and career.

Camille Paglia, Social activist

278.

Be bold. If you're going to make an error, make a doozey, and don't be afraid to hit the ball.

Billie Jean King, Athlete

279.

When I was a little girl my grandmother – who was in her early seventies – would say: "Child you're black and you are going to be a woman and I don't think you can change either one of the two. But you are bright and you have a brain. Use it to show them you are coming through."

Shirley Chisholm, Congresswoman

280.

Ego is a killer. Humility is probably the greatest power that one can study, to understand that you didn't create anything here … I feel that if you study humility in your work, in your life, you will be studying the power of success.

Melba Moore, Singer

281.

I look back on my life like a good day's work; it is done, and I am satisfied with it.

Grandma Moses, Painter

282.

Nothing is easy to the unwilling.

Nikki Giovanni, Poet

282.

Do not be afraid of mistakes, providing you do not make the same one twice.

Eleanor Roosevelt, First Lady

284.

You need to get up in the morning and say, "Boy, I'm going to—in my own stupid way—save the world today."

Carol Bellamy, Entrepreneur

285.

Why, I feel so tall within—I feel as if the power of a nation is within me!

Sojourner Truth, Women's Rights Activist

286.

If you have made mistakes, even serious ones, there is always another chance for you. What we call failure is not the falling down, but the staying down.

Mary Pickford, Actor

297.

No matter what accomplishments you make, somebody helps you.

Althea Gibson, Tennis Player

288.

I just take one day. Yesterday is gone.
Tomorrow has not come. We have only
today to love Jesus.

Mother Teresa, Humanitarian

289.

It takes great passion and great energy to
do anything creative, especially in the
theater. You have to care so much that
you can't sleep, you can't eat, you can't
talk to people. It's just got to be right.
You can't do it without that passion.

Agnes DeMille, Dancer

291.

We plant seeds that will flower as results
in our lives, so best to remove the weeds
of anger, avarice, envy and doubt...

Dorothy Day, Social activist

292.

Sometimes I would almost rather have people take away years of my life than take away a moment.

Pearl Bailey, Singer

293.

Most of us measure our success by what others haven't done.

Tina Turner, Singer

294.

The most valuable gift I ever received was ... the gift of insecurity ... my father left us. My mother's love might not have prepared me for life the way my father's departure did. He forced us out on the road, where we had to earn our bread.

Lillian Gish, Actor

295.

Challenges make you discover things about yourself that you never really knew. They're what make the instrument stretch, what make you go beyond the norm.

Cicely Tyson, Actor

296.

Even though people may be well known, they hold in their hearts the emotions of a simple person for the moments that are the most important of those we know on earth: birth, marriage and death.

Jacqueline Kennedy Onassis, First Lady

297.

Every man is free to rise as far as he's able or willing, but the degree to which he thinks determines the degree to which he'll rise.

Ayn Rand, Writer

298.

Love the moment, and the energy of that moment will spread beyond all boundaries.

Corita Kent, Graphic Artist

299.

I love the challenge of starting at zero every day and seeing how much I can accomplish.

Martha Stewart, Entrepreneur

300.

Being powerful is like being a lady. If you have to tell people you are, you aren't.

Margaret Thatcher, Prime Minister

301.

Like you, I'm still a work in progress. And the next step beyond failure could be your biggest success.

Debbie Allen, Dancer

302.

I don't know anything about luck. I've never banked on it, and I'm afraid of people who do. Luck to me is something else: hard work and realizing what is opportunity and what isn't.

Lucille Ball, Comedian

303.

I didn't have anybody, really, no foundation in life, so I had to make my own way. Always. From the start. I had to go out in the world and become strong ...

Tina Turner, Singer

304.

I'm no martyr. I just had a hard day at work. My feet were hurting, and I was too tired to give up my seat.

Rosa Parks, Civil Rights Activist

305.

Misery is a communicable disease.

Martha Graham, Dancer

306.

I have always grown from my problems and challenges, from the things that don't work out. That's when I've really learned.

Carol Burnett, Comedian

307.

To feel valued, to know, even if only once in a while, that you can do a job well is an absolutely marvelous feeling.

Barbara Walters, Journalist

308.

There's no free lunch. Don't feel entitled to anything you don't sweat and struggle for.

Marian Wright Edelman, Educator

309.

Measure not the work until the day's out and the labor done.

Elizabeth Barrett Browning, Poet

310.

Establishing lasting peace is the work of education; all politics can do is keep us out of war.

Maria Montessori, Educator

311.

Integrate what you believe into every single area of your life. Take your heart to work and ask the most and best of everybody else. Don't let your special character and values, the secret that you know and no one else does, the truth—don't let that get swallowed up by the great chewing complacency.

Meryl Streep, Actor

312.

Nothing is interesting if you're not interested.

Helen MacInness, Author

313.

I make the most of all that comes and the least of all that goes.

Sara Teasdale, Poet

314.

I have worked all my life, wanted to work all my life, needed to work all my life.

Liz Carpenter, Writer

315.

I like people who refuse to speak until they are ready to speak.

Lillian Hellman, Playwright

316.

I don't care how many times you hear the word no. You ain't gonna give up. Either live North or die!

Harriet Tubman, Conductor, Underground Railroad

317.

The young do not know enough to be prudent, and therefore they attempt the impossible – and achieve it, generation after generation.

Pearl S. Buck, Writer

318.

It doesn't matter what you're trying to accomplish. It's all a matter of discipline … I was determined to discover what life held for me beyond the inner-city streets.

Wilma Rudolph, Olympian

319.

I believe one thing: that today is yesterday and tomorrow is today and you can't stop.

Martha Graham, Dancer

320.

The main reason I wanted to be successful was to get out of the ghetto. My parents helped direct my path.

Florence Griffith-Joyner, Olympian

321.

Defining myself, as opposed to being defined by others, is one of the most difficult challenges I face.

Carol Moseley-Braun, Senator

322.

My grandfather once told me that there were two kinds of people: those who do the work and those who take the credit. He told me to try to be in the first group; there was much less competition.

Indira Gandhi, Prime Minister

323.

My epitaph should read: "She worked herself into this ground."

Kay Bailey Huchinson, Senator

324.

My recipe for life is not being afraid of myself, afraid of what I think, or of my opinions.

Eartha Kitt, Singer

325.

Aerodynamically the bumblebee shouldn't be able to fly, but the bumblebee doesn't know it so it goes on flying anyway.

Mary Kay Ash, Entrepreneur

326.

There are no hopeless situations; there are only men who have grown hopeless about them.

Clare Boothe Luce, Diplomat

327.

It's not what you do once in a while,
It's what you do day in and day out
That makes the difference.

Jenny Craig, Entrepreneur

328.

It's better to look ahead and prepare than
to look back and regret.

Jackie Joyner Kersee, Olympian

329.

Success has made failures of many men.

Cindy Adams, Journalist

330.

My mother taught me very early to
believe I could achieve any
accomplishment I wanted to. The first was
to walk without braces.

Wilma Rudolph, Olympian

331.

Whatever muscles I have are the product of my own hard work and nothing else.

Evelyn Ashford, Olympian

332.

I want to do it because I want to do it. Women must try to do things as men have tried. When they fail, their failure must be but a challenge to others.

Amelia Earhart, Pilot

333.

Hope is the thing with feathers that perches in the soul and sings the tune without words and never stops at all.

Emily Dickinson, Poet

334.

Let nothing disturb you. Let nothing frighten you. Everything passes away except God.

Saint Theresa of Jesus

335.

Father, I beg of Thee a little task
To dignify my days, 'tis all I ask.

Edna St. Vicent Millay, Poet

336.

People who fight fire with fire usually
end up with ashes.

Abigail Van Buren, Writer

337.

Some of us aren't prepared to accept
success—especially someone else's.

Sarah Vaughan, Singer

338.

I've always believed that one woman's
success can only help another woman's
success.

Gloria Vanderbilt, Artist

339.

One filled with joy preaches without preaching.

Mother Teresa, Humanitarian

340.

Changes are not predictable; but to deny them is to be an accomplice to one's own unnecessary vegetation.

Gail Sheehy, Writer

341.

Why hate when you could spend your time doing other things?

Miriam Makeba, Singer

342.

Decide on what you think is right, and stick to it.

George Eliot, Writer

343.

I really, deeply believe that dreams do come true. Often, they might not come when you want them. They come in their own time.

Diana Ross, Singer

344.

We all live with the objective of being happy; our lives are all different and yet the same.

Anne Frank, Writer

345.

Getting ahead in a difficult profession requires avid faith in yourself. That is why some people with mediocre talent, but with great inner drive, go much further than people with vastly superior talent.

Sophia Loren, Actor

346.

Class is an aura of confidence that is being sure without being cocky. Class has nothing to do with money. Class never runs scared. It is self-discipline and self-knowledge. It's the sure-footedness that comes with having proved you can meet life.

Ann Landers, Writer

347.

Starting out to make money is the greatest mistake in life. Do what you feel you have a flair for doing, and if you are good enough at it, the money will come.

Greer Garson, Actor

348.

The success of life, the formation of character, is in proportion to the courage one has to say to one's ownself: "Thou shalt not."

Carry Nation, Prohibitionist

349.

If you just set out to be liked, you would be prepared to compromise on anything at any time, and you would achieve nothing.

Margaret Thatcher, Prime Minister

350.

The skilled woman can invent beauty over and over again with extraordinary effect. The art of inventing beauty transcends class, intellect, age, profession, geography – virtually every cultural and economic barrier.

Estee Lauder, Entrepreneur

351.

We can do no great things—only small things with great love.

Mother Teresa, Humanitarian

352.

It seems to me we can never give up longing
and wishing while we are alive. There are
certain things we feel to be beautiful and
good, and we must hunger for them.

George Eliot, Writer

353.

No life is so hard that you can't make it
easier by the way you take it.

Ellen Glasgow, Author

354.

If only we'd stop trying to be happy we'd
have a pretty good time.

Edith Wharton, Writer

355.

The moment somebody says to me, "This
is very risky," is the moment it becomes
attractive to me.

Kate Capshaw, Actor

356.

Did I pay my dues? You bet. Was it tough? Without a doubt. But I was determined to find out how high is high!

Halle Berry, Actor

357.

You're as happy as you allow yourself to be—so why be unhappy?

Marilyn Quayle, Attorney

358.

What I wanted to be when I grew up was – in charge.

Wilma Vaught, Brigadier General, USAF

359.

An aim in life is the only fortune worth finding.

Jacqueline Kennedy Onassis, First Lady

360.

Humility is no substitute for a good personality.

Fran Lebowitz, Writer

361.

A positive attitude can really make dreams come true - it did for me.

Zina Garrison, Tennis Player

362.

To have a reason to get up in the morning, it is necessary to possess a guiding principle. A belief of some kind. A bumper sticker, if you will.

Judith Guest, Writer

363.

Remember, Ginger Rogers did everything Fred Astaire did, but she did it backwards and in high heels.

Faith Whittlesey, Ambassador

364.

I'm not happy, I'm cheerful. There's a difference. A happy woman has no cares at all. A cheerful woman has cares but has learned how to deal with them.

Beverly Sills, Opera Singer

365.

Everything's in the mind. That's where it all starts. Knowing what you want is the first step toward getting it.

Mae West, Actor

Become an Action Principles Champion™

"How wonderful it is that nobody need wait a moment before starting to improve the world."
Anne Frank

The philosophy underlying the Action Principles® is self-improvement and service to others. If you believe in this message, you will want to share Action Principles® books with other women. You become the teacher. You become the motivator.

Throughout our books, course and videos, we refer to Action Principles Champions™. These are our members. In large part, our nonprofit work is support by those who join us by becoming Champions. It's simple. When you buy and distribute one hundred books copies of any of our pocket sized motivational books, you become an Action Principles Champion™. We will acknowledge your Championship contribution with a certificate suitable for framing.

Give books to acquaintances and leave books anonymously in public places. Think of a woman in crisis who happens to find your Action Principles® book. Although you may never personally know the recipient of your book, that woman will know that someone cared and God will know of your selfless effort. You make the world a better place.

In advance, our Champions, we thank you.

Championship Offer

Motivate!

Share with:

Be a Champion Family
Friends
Students
Co-workers

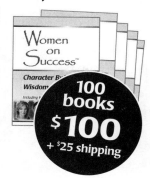

Women on Success™

Character B...
Wisdom

100 books $100
+ $25 shipping

Bonus Books Free

You will also receive: Positive Mental Attitudes
• The Action Principles • Sports Legends on
Success • African-Americans on Success and a
complete library of Action Principles Posters
Four books and ten posters – free!

To Order Online: Success.org/order
Phone: 800-585-1300
Fax: 508-653-2924
Email: orders@Success.org
Mail: ASI, 5 N Main St., Natick, MA 01760

119

Be the Motivator!
Be the Teacher!

Our pocket-sized books are the perfect little gifts, which show others that you sincerely want the best for them. They are motivational tools for you to begin positive conversations with your children, students, employees or athletes. Leave a book anonymously in a public place and your act may change a stranger's life. Your generosity and compassion make the world a better place. Read more about these books on Success.org. Call, fax, email or mail your order, today. Thank you.

120

The Women's Discussion Forum

On Success.org

Mentor Teach Learn Discuss

As a successful woman, a survivor, a leader, we need your insights and ideas. We ask you to post and share your wit and wisdom with the international  Success.org community. All topics are welcomed from business to relationships to politics to personal development and finding life's balance. Your thoughts and sentiments might just help another woman in a time of need. Have a concern? Ask a question and you may receive just the advice you need to solve a problem or facilitate a project. Share with others on Success.org.

When you reach one hundred or more posts, you will become an Action Principles Champion™ and receive a free framed certificate acknowledging your contribution to help others.

Free Women's Empowerment Course

On Success.org

MASTER SUCCESS

Put purpose, passion, prosperity and peace into your life. Take control. Find balance. Learn when to say, "Yes," and how to say, "No." Bring forth the courage, confidence and leadership abilities found in the style and attitudes of all women committed to self-improvement and service. This is success. Respect and appreciation will be yours.

This course brings the Action Principles® to life and may be one of the most rewarding courses you will ever take. Master Success is a simple, direct, life-affirming system for those willing to do the work to have it all. The course is based on Bill FitzPatrick's best selling book, *Master Success*. Video support, student forum, resources and links.

Free Women's Empowerment Course

On Success.org

MASTER SMALL BUSINESS

Women-owned businesses account for 28 percent of all privately-owned businesses in the United States, employing 9.2 million people. Women contribute $2.38 trillion in revenue every year to the U.S. economy!

Why not be the boss? Find the new independent self-reliant you. You can do it all. You can have it all. Pay your bills. Spoil those you love. Invest for a comfortable future.

Would you like to start your own business? Expand an existing business? Receive a promotion? Be a more valuable employee? Start part-time? Work from home? Business Week Magazine said this course "provides gentle entry for any intimidated would-be entrepreneur." Recommended by the Small Business Administration. 30-lesson interactive course packed with practical ideas and stories of successful women in business. Tens of thousands of students worldwide. International edition, "How Do Americans Get Rich?" Video support, student forum, resources and links.

Free Women's Empowerment Course

On Success.org

MASTER SELF DEFENSE

Don't be a victim. Bill FitzPatrick is a Shaolin Master, a 5th degree black belt in Kempo karate. He loves to advance the warrior spirit and teach

the martial arts. Bill has enlisted the help of many of the nation's top martial arts instructors in bringing this course to the public during these challenging times. Learn how to be self-confident, aware, and to defend yourself and loved ones. This online course is especially important for women and seniors. Topics include how to be safe at home, school, work, in the community and while traveling. Presented in cooperation with our sister website, Dojo.com. Video support, student forum, resources and links.

Free Women's Empowerment Course

On Success.org

MASTER REAL ESTATE

Millions of American women buy real estate every year. They're smart. Join them.

Take charge of your own financial future. Work for twenty years and retire. Would you like to own your own home or condo? Would you like to invest in real estate? This ten-lesson system for investing in local real estate will get you started. This system works anywhere and under all economic conditions. If you know anyone who will ever buy or sell a house, rent an apartment, store or office, encourage her to take this course. Take action. Buy six properties and love your tenants. Video support, student forum, resources and links.

American Success Institute, Inc.

The American Success Institute (ASI) is a 501(c)3 non-profit educational and philanthropic organization founded in 1993 by Bill FitzPatrick. The mission of ASI is to create a worldwide community in which all members are fully involved participants living and encouraging the expansion of the Action Principle® ideals of self-improvement and service based on established religious faith.

SUCCESS.org

Success.org is ASI's multi-media interactive website featuring free courses on business and personal development. Students visiting the site will find resource materials, discussion forums and ways to join us in our work.

Many national and world leaders have contributed to our Action Principles® Leadership Project.

About Dojo.com

FREE. The mission of Dojo.com is to empower motivated students around the world with the confidence and practical skills necessary to deal effectively with security and self-defense situations. Promoting peace through understanding, goodwill and strength. This interactive multimedia site features the Master Self-Defense Course, martial arts ebooks, video instruction, cartoons, student forums, Masters Hall of Fame, links and resources. This site is for karate students, women, seniors and anyone interested in the martial arts.

About CatholicActionPrinciples.com

FREE. Guided by the Catholic faith, you can choose to live a joyous life of prosperity and peace. Features the *Catholic Action Principles*™ [English and Spanish] with contributions from many cardinals, bishops and other religious leaders. A peace resource section, teachers guide, tools for evangelists and an interactive forum are included.

Help Empower Other Women

Link Your Website to Success.org

There are over seventy-eight million entries for the word "success" on Google, Success.org is #1. There are good reasons for women to tell other women about Success.org.

FREE. The Action Principles® over 3 million copies in print and online. Available in 18 languages.

FREE. The Master Success Courses™ show women all the potential they have to choose full lives of purpose, passion, prosperity and peace.

FREE. The Women's Discussion Forum gives women an opportunity to share their ideas on positive living.

FREE. *Women on Success*™ is available as a continually updated and expanded e-book on Success.org.

FREE. Women's Leadership Project. A growing archive of Women's Action Principles™ contributed by prominent women in government, religion, business, education, the military, and the arts.

Linking your website to Success.org gives your website visitors the opportunity to discover the free educational offerings on Success.org. Your effort will be respected and appreciated. Linking your website is easy, details and graphic options on Success.org.